Remembering Our Queen

The Illustrated
Story of
Queen Elizabeth II

Remembering Our Queen

The Illustrated Story of Queen Elizabeth II

written by

Smriti Prasadam-Halls

illustrated by

Kim Geyer & Josie Shenoy

wren
&rook

Contents

Introduction

At 6.30 p.m. on 8 September 2022, Buckingham Palace announced that Queen Elizabeth II had died. It was the end of an era. At the age of 96, the Queen had been alive for longer than most of the British population and had been on the throne for many people's whole lives.

Queen Elizabeth II was the longest reigning monarch in British history. Her reign (1952–2022) spanned seventy years of huge political and social change across the world, as well as giant leaps in technology, medicine and science.

Already a mother of two when she became queen, Elizabeth II provided the world with an incredible example of a capable, strong woman and working mum leading a powerful country at a time when that was rare. She was a national role model on an international stage, inspiring women and girls the world over.

As you'll discover in the pages of this book, the Queen dedicated herself to serving her people around the world and supporting efforts to bring peace, justice and equality. Although the pain and impact from Britain's colonial past is still felt by many today, she sought to bring countries and people together in friendship.

You will see that she was a woman of great faith who welcomed people of all religions, and that she encouraged everyone to play their part for the common good and for the protection of the environment. You will find out how she herself served in the Second World War and how she sought to keep the flames of remembrance alight throughout her reign.

Spending seventy years on the throne, the Queen became a bridge between past and present and inspired deep affection and respect amongst many. Much cherished, Queen Elizabeth II holds a very special place in the hearts of people all around the world.

Together, we remember her remarkable life.

The Monarchy

The United Kingdom is a type of monarchy. This is a system where power and authority for a country are held by one ruler – a responsibility that lasts for their whole life.

The monarchy has existed in Britain for over 1,000 years and the role of monarch is passed down through families. The Queen became monarch in 1952, a year before her coronation, when her father King George VI died.

In the past, the monarch played a powerful part in governing the country. Today, although the monarch remains head of state, the United Kingdom is a constitutional monarchy. This puts the power for passing laws and the day-to-day running of the country in the hands of the government. The people of the country choose their government by electing them into power.

Queen Elizabeth II was not only queen of the United Kingdom, she was monarch of fifteen countries at the end of her reign. These are known as the Commonwealth realms. She was also head of both the church and army, holding the titles of Supreme Governor of the Church of England, Defender of the Faith and Commander-in-Chief of the British Armed Forces.

DIEU DROIT ET MON

The Queen was in daily contact with the government through the delivery of the red box, a briefcase containing documents for her to read and sign. International relations were a key part of her role and the Queen worked hard to represent the best of Britain. Travelling all over the world, she created and maintained valuable relationships with other countries, ensuring that Britain stayed on good terms with them.

The role of monarch is steeped in pomp and pageantry and traditions that date back centuries. However, the most important role of the monarch is to act as a symbol of unity and stability for the nation.

Queen Elizabeth stood for the values that she held dear. This was never more evident than at times of crisis and of celebration.

The Queen frequently hosted dinners at Buckingham Palace for world leaders who visited Britain.

Queen Elizabeth's Family Tree

There was much cooing and excitement on 21 April 1926
when a royal baby girl was born to the Duke and Duchess of York.
No one dreamt that little Princess Elizabeth would one day be queen.

The little princess was a direct descendant of William the Conqueror
and a great-great-granddaughter of Queen Victoria and Prince Albert.

After Victoria's death in 1901, her son became King Edward VII.
He was married to a Danish princess called Alexandra, and after
he died in 1910, his son George V took the throne with his
wife Queen Mary. This was the beginning of the House of
Windsor and it was George V who was king when
Princess Elizabeth was born. Elizabeth called
him 'Grandpa England'.

George V's eldest son was next to become king, Edward VIII, but his reign lasted less than a year. The woman he wished to marry had been married before and, as king, Edward wasn't permitted to marry anyone who had been divorced. To the astonishment of the nation, Edward chose to abdicate and his shy younger brother, known as Bertie, became King George VI in 1936.

George VI and Queen Elizabeth were Princess Elizabeth's parents. They were well liked and won people's respect by remaining in London throughout the bombing raids of the Second World War.

The people were also keen to know whatever they could about the King's eldest daughter, Elizabeth – the little girl who would one day be queen.

The young princess was known to her close family as Lilibet.

Her Majesty's Childhood

Princess Elizabeth was very close to her family and, at first, she lived a quiet life with her sister Margaret and their parents in Mayfair, London. The princesses were taught their lessons at home by a governess and also learned how to sing, dance and speak French.

Princess Elizabeth loved animals, especially corgis. She loved horses too, and before long had become an accomplished rider.

As soon as her father became king, the family moved to Buckingham Palace. It was large, grand and imposing, and life here felt very different for the young princesses. But the King was determined that his daughters would still be sociable and so a special troop of the Girl Guides was created at the palace.

GIRL GUIDES

Elizabeth was thirteen when the Second World War broke out. Bombs rained down on London and sirens screeched. The princesses were taken to the safety of Windsor Castle and it was from here that the future queen gave her first speech to the nation.

Over the radio, she sent a heartfelt message of reassurance to children being evacuated to the countryside, telling them that she knew how it felt to be 'away from those we love most of all'.

Her words were very welcome. In a few short sentences, she had given the country a glimpse of the leader she would become.

A leader who would do her duty, take her position seriously and who cared deeply for the people of her country.

When Princess Elizabeth was seven, she was given a pet corgi, which she named Dookie.

The Queen in the Second World War

Beep beep! A horn tooted loudly as a military ambulance pulled up.
At the wheel was Second Subaltern Elizabeth Alexandra Mary Windsor.

Princess Elizabeth spent her teenage years growing up against the backdrop of the Second World War. Like so many other young people, she desperately wanted to play her part in the war effort. Once she was eighteen, she persuaded her parents to let her join the Auxiliary Territorial Service (ATS). Quick, capable and clever, the princess learned how to drive lorries and ambulances, read maps, change wheels and repair engines.

On 8 May 1945, when the war in Europe finally ended, Princess Elizabeth appeared on the balcony of Buckingham Palace, dressed proudly in her ATS uniform. As evening drew in, the mechanic-princess slipped into the crowds with her sister, unnoticed, and joined the celebration.

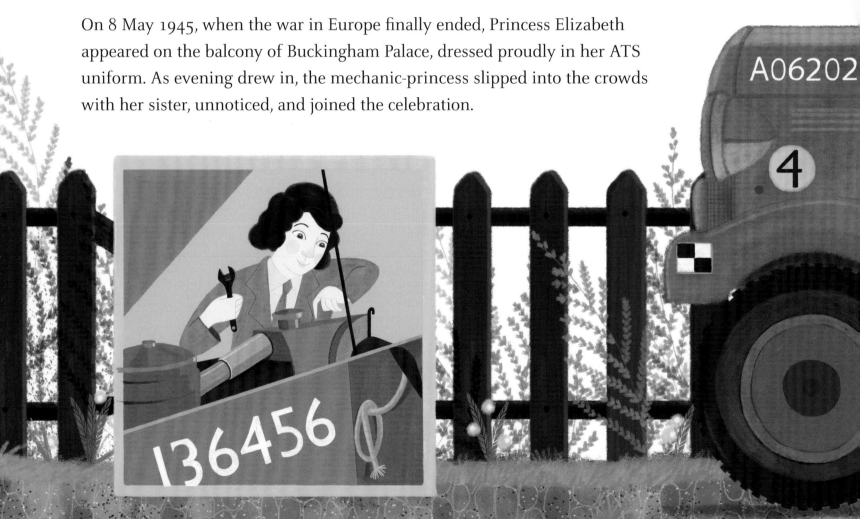

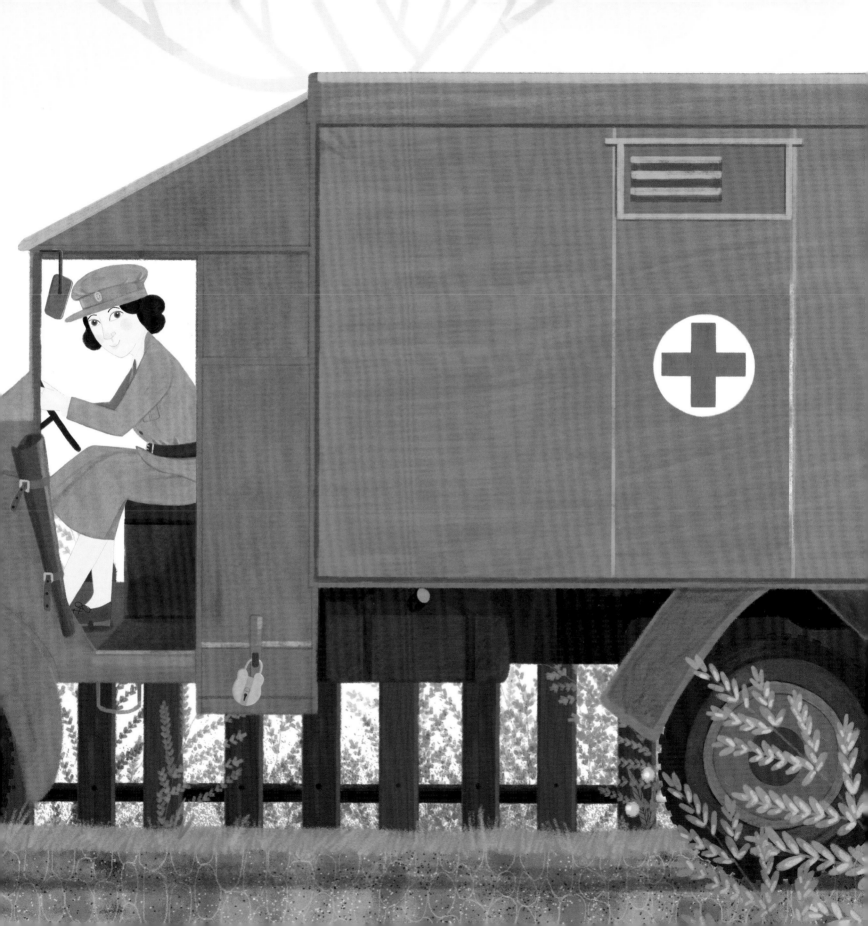

The Coronation

Rain drummed down on the spires of Westminster Abbey
in London, but inside there was pin-drop silence as
Princess Elizabeth was crowned Queen Elizabeth II.

Her voice rang out, clear and confident, as she solemnly gave her oath
to serve the people of the United Kingdom of Great Britain and
Northern Ireland, and the countries of the Commonwealth.

It was 2 June 1953 and all eyes were on Elizabeth. There were 8,000 guests
in the abbey, many thousands more lining the streets in jubilation,
and millions watching on television from their own homes.

The coronation was the first-ever public ceremony to be televised.
Young Queen Elizabeth, only 27 years old, wanted to give *all* her people
a chance to share in the splendour of the day with her.

A modern queen for modern times.

The Commonwealth

It was January 1961 and the air was filled with the sweet scent of flowers. The Queen and her husband, Prince Philip, bowing their heads in respect, laid a wreath of 500 white roses at the memorial to Mahatma Gandhi in Delhi, India.

It was deeply symbolic that the Queen chose to make the first engagement of her first-ever visit to India to pay her respects to Gandhi, the man who had led India's independence movement and been imprisoned for his opposition to British rule. This simple act earned her admiration from many people in India.

Later that year, during a visit to Ghana, the Queen danced the foxtrot with Ghana's first president, Kwame Nkrumah, another independence leader formerly imprisoned for his efforts to win his country's freedom.

Britain once ruled many countries as part of a large empire, but gradually many of those countries have gained independence. Throughout her reign, the Queen sought to build peace and friendship between Britain and the newly independent nations. She embraced their independence and celebrated their flourishing nationhood.

Many of these countries, including India and Ghana, now belong to the Commonwealth, which is a voluntary group of 56 countries. The Queen was head of the Commonwealth. Unlike her position as queen, this was not a role she inherited from her father, but one for which she was chosen by the Commonwealth's member countries.

Today's Commonwealth includes wealthy countries and developing countries. It includes some of the world's most heavily populated countries as well as some of its smallest.

Regardless of their size or their wealth, the Commonwealth is based on the principle that all member states are equal to each other and will work together towards the shared goals of prosperity, democracy and peace.

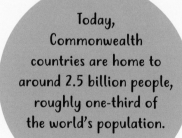

Today, Commonwealth countries are home to around 2.5 billion people, roughly one-third of the world's population.

Commonwealth Flag

19

The Queen at Home

Mother, grandmother, great-grandmother, daughter, sister and wife. Elizabeth II had many titles she cherished in addition to her royal ones.

She always valued family life, but her family life wasn't always smooth. The Queen described 1992 as her horrible year, because so many things seemed to have gone wrong. In doing so, she demonstrated that although queen, she still shared some of the same troubles and sadness that many families experience.

Elizabeth II was already a parent of two small children, Charles and Anne, when she came to the throne, and had two more in the years that followed. Queen Elizabeth was a working mother for all seven decades of her reign, setting a fine example of a strong female leader who was respected, admired and loved – both abroad and at home.

Lover of Corgis

Wife

Mother

Sister

Longest-serving monarch

Equestrian

The 1950s

Tongan melodies were carried on a fresh sea breeze that blew gently through the open sides of a cool, white canopy. The Queen and Prince Philip sat cross-legged before a sumptuous banquet of roast pig, lobster and watermelon served on smooth, green banana leaves.

Their host was Queen Salote. Earlier that year, she had travelled over 16,000 kilometres to attend the Queen's coronation and Queen Elizabeth had insisted that she return the visit during her first – and longest – royal tour, which lasted six months in all, spanning 1953 and 1954.

From Tonga, the Queen travelled on to Australia, where she spent eight weeks touring the whole country. It is believed that three-quarters of all Australians turned out in person to catch sight of the Queen during that trip.

These two visits captured the Queen's fresh approach to the role of the monarch in countries of the Commonwealth, moving from a relationship based on empire to one seeking equality.

Similar changes were slowly taking place across 1950s Britain. Following the Second World War, Britain encouraged immigration from Commonwealth countries. Over the next twenty years, more than 500,000 people from India, Pakistan and across Africa and the Caribbean arrived in Britain on ships like the *Empire Windrush*, determined to help rebuild the country after the war.

They came at the invitation of the UK government, but sadly many were often made to feel unwelcome. However, in the decades to come, their traditions and heritage would help shape Britain's cultural life, influencing music, literature, food, film, fashion and much more. Professionally, their hard work would contribute greatly to enriching post-war, cosmopolitan Britain in all areas, and help to strengthen and staff the fledgling NHS.

Change was coming and the Queen was modelling friendship and respect among peoples and nations.

In 1953, just days before the Queen's coronation, Tenzing Norgay and Edmund Hillary became the first people to reach the summit of Mount Everest after seven weeks of climbing.

A year later, in 1954, Roger Bannister, a medical student at a London hospital, became the first person to run a mile in less than four minutes. It was a remarkable moment in the history of sport.

The 1960s

It was the decade when the first person walked on the moon and when England famously won the football World Cup – with the Queen presenting the trophy to the England Team at Wembley. Anything seemed possible. The 'Swinging Sixties' were an exciting period of great social change. New laws were passed giving people more freedom to live and love as they chose.

Progress was also being made on winning women's rights. Demands for equal pay and equal chances to work were beginning to be heard. And it was at this moment that the Queen added her own voice to calls for change . . .

On Christmas Day 1966, as families settled down in front of their television sets, paper crowns perched on their heads and tummies filled with roast turkey, the Queen delivered a Christmas message celebrating the major role played by women in society and praising their efforts to take up their full part in public life.

She noted that:

'. . . it has been women who have breathed gentleness and care into the harsh progress of mankind. The struggles against inhuman prejudice, against squalor, ignorance, and disease, have always owed a great deal to the determination and tenacity of women . . . In the modern world the opportunities for women to give something of value to the human family are greater than ever.'

The Queen ended her broadcast with a prayer that everyone should find the personal strength 'to build a world that will be a happier and more peaceful place in which to live.'

With these powerful words, the Queen demonstrated how much she wanted women everywhere to feel her support and her deep admiration.

In the sixties, Britain's young people found the creativity and confidence to explore many new forms of music, art and fashion.

The Queen's Honours

The grand gates of Buckingham Palace swung open as world-famous band The Beatles arrived to receive their medals of honour from the Queen. Screaming fans thronged the streets outside.

The Royal Honours are announced twice a year and consist of many different medals. The best known are the MBE, OBE, CBE and the KBE/DBE – also known as a knighthood or damehood. They are presented at a special ceremony at one of the royal palaces.

Some recipients are well-known figures like actors, sportspeople and musicians, but many more are extraordinary everyday people celebrated for charity work or for their contribution to the arts, medicine, faith, science, literature and the wider community.

Not everyone who is chosen wishes to accept, but for those that do, it's a special and rare mark of recognition.

The 1970s

The air was still, and bright sunshine bathed the Queen in warm light as she chatted with Mairead Corrigan and Betty Williams.

Visiting Northern Ireland as part of her Silver Jubilee tour, the Queen had asked to meet these two remarkable women. They had been awarded the Nobel Peace Prize the previous year for their efforts to bring communities together and to end fighting that had been causing so much pain in Northern Ireland.

Together, Mairead and Betty had started an organisation called the Peace People, whose aim was 'to live and love and build a just and peaceful society'. The organisation held big marches in which hundreds of thousands of people took part, all calling for peace. After the creation of the Peace People, fewer people died as a result of the fighting.

Peace movements were taking place throughout the 1970s, influencing politics and culture. As the Queen left Northern Ireland, she spoke of her own prayers for reconciliation and understanding, and her hopes for people to work together in friendship and forgiveness to bring peace.

Three decades later, Elizabeth II would become the first UK monarch to visit the Republic of Ireland.

She was praised for her contribution to the peace process, helping to repair relationships between neighbours and nations.

Always one to keep up with new technologies, the Queen was one of the very first heads of state to send an email. She sent her first message in 1976 – many years before most people had even heard of electronic mail.

The 1970s also saw decimalisation, with Britain changing its money. Instead of 240 pennies in a pound, there were now just 100 new pence. But the new coins still had a picture of the Queen's head on one side.

Meanwhile, Concorde – the supersonic passenger plane – began regular service, flying from London to New York in just under three hours, reaching speeds of over 2,000 kph. The Queen became a frequent passenger using Concorde on three separate visits to Barbados.

The Queen's Christmas Broadcast

Christmas lights twinkled and baubles shone brightly from the festive tree . . . lights, camera, action!

The Queen's Christmas Broadcast was viewed by millions around the world each year and regularly topped the UK viewing ratings. It was first transmitted by radio, before becoming televised in 1957. Gathering round to listen formed an essential part of Christmas traditions for many, and the message was pre-recorded so it could be aired in all Commonwealth countries on Christmas Day.

In her message, the Queen reflected on important events of the year, both public and personal, and anchored her thoughts in the Christian message which lies at the heart of the festival, often speaking of forgiveness and love for others.

Hopeful, kind and all-embracing, it was always a message of peace and goodwill for everyone.

The 1980s

The mighty dome of St Paul's Cathedral resounded with organ music.
It was the Royal Wedding of 1981 and the Queen's eldest son,
Prince Charles, was getting married to Lady Diana Spencer.

Princess Diana shared the Queen's passion for helping others. She
became well known for her charity work, reaching out to some
of the world's most overlooked and vulnerable people.

The 1980s saw a growing interest in helping those in need and it
marked the beginning of very large, very popular fundraising events.
Charities that are household names today – such as Children in Need and
Comic Relief – began work, encouraging everyone to do their little bit to
raise money for those who were disadvantaged or living in poverty.

A rock concert called Live Aid was held in July 1985 to raise money for those suffering from a terrible famine in Ethiopia. It was broadcast in 110 countries and watched across the globe. The concert was a huge success, raising around £30 million and viewed by around 1.9 billion people – about 40% of the world's population at the time.

In a decade where some people had plenty and others did not, the Queen continued to support the efforts of all those trying to make a difference. On a visit to India in 1983, she presented Mother Teresa of Kolkata with the Order of Merit to honour her outstanding service in helping others.

She later quoted words from Mother Teresa: 'Not all of us can do great things – but we can do small things with great love.'

The Royal Wedding in 1981 was watched by 750 million people. It was the biggest televised event since the Queen's coronation.

The Queen and Her Faith

Lambeth Palace was filled with lively, warm chatter. Leaders from nine different faiths were gathered to show the Queen beautiful, sacred objects and holy texts from their traditions as part of her Diamond Jubilee celebration.

The Queen was a devout and practising Christian and, as head of the Church of England, held the title Defender of the Faith. It was always clear to see that her own deep faith was at the heart of all she did. She spoke often about how she put her trust in God to guide her through good times and bad.

The Queen used her faith to embrace people of other faiths and none, offering them the same respect and dignity as those who shared her own beliefs.

The 1990s

Pop music filled the Royal Albert Hall, but it could only just be heard above the excited cheering of the audience. Up in the Royal Box, to the delight of all the guests, Nelson Mandela stood up and started dancing to the rhythms of the British and South African artists on stage. Then, to the surprise of all assembled, the Queen rose to her feet to enjoy the music too.

The Queen had a very warm friendship with the first democratically elected president of South Africa. Nelson Mandela had been imprisoned for 27 years under a system of racial discrimination called apartheid, which kept white and non-white people separated through strict laws. The Queen gave her personal support and encouragement to the efforts of Commonwealth leaders to force the end of apartheid and white-minority rule in South Africa. Mandela's release was a source of great joy for her. In 1995, she awarded him the prestigious Order of Merit.

In a break with formal custom, Nelson Mandela was the only person from outside the Royal Family allowed to call Her Majesty by her first name. Their affection for each other was based on mutual respect and admiration.

Connections were being made closer to home as well. In an impressive feat of engineering, the Channel Tunnel physically joined Britain to mainland Europe. After the opening ceremony in France, the Queen became the first official passenger on board a train through the tunnel, back to the UK.

In 1993 Buckingham Palace opened its grand doors to the public for the first time. Visitors poured in and within one week, tickets to view the majestic rooms had booked up for the next three years.

Bridges were being built within and between countries, both physical and social. As the new millennium approached, the world was changing fast and the Queen was fully on board.

In 1993 the World Wide Web became available to the public. There was an explosion in its popularity, with the Queen soon joining the fast-growing trend and launching the royal website in 1997. By the end of the decade, 130 million people around the world were using the internet.

Commonwealth Games

Cheers erupted as the athletes entered the stadium. Waving their national flags proudly, the young competitors from around the globe embodied a spirit of excellence, dedication and immense talent.

Begun in 1930, the Commonwealth Games is a twelve-day festival of sport that takes place every four years in a different Commonwealth city. These have included Kuala Lumpur, Delhi, Melbourne, Manchester, Cardiff, Vancouver, Glasgow and Birmingham.

A special message from the Queen would open the ceremony. It would be hidden inside a baton, which had made its way to every Commonwealth country in a ten-month relay.

Celebratory and truly inclusive, the Commonwealth Games are the only major international games to include para-sports in the main events, and to give an equal number of medals to both women and men.

The 2000s

The sky above Buckingham Palace and The Mall was a sea of scarlet as one million poppies fluttered silently to the ground. They were released by a Lancaster bomber which roared overhead, accompanied by two other fighter planes – a Spitfire and a Hurricane. This special moment was part of the sixtieth anniversary commemoration for the end of the Second World War.

Following a lunch for war veterans, a parade up the Mall and a two-minute silence to remember all the British and Commonwealth soldiers who sacrificed their lives, buglers of the Indian Army performed the 'Last Post'. It was a moving reminder of the 2.5 million Indians who fought in the war alongside their British comrades – as well as the part played by the Gurkhas and so many forgotten soldiers from other Commonwealth countries, such as Nigeria, Jamaica and Australia, who served on behalf of the British Army in both world wars.

Just three days before the sixtieth anniversary celebration, London itself had been rocked by a series of terrorist bombs. In her speech to the veterans, the Queen asked Londoners to follow the example set by the wartime generation – an example of resilience, humour and courage.

Giving honour and respect to those who serve their country was always very important to the Queen. Each Remembrance Sunday, she led the nation in remembering those who have died in wars and other conflicts. She would lay a wreath of poppies at the foot of the Cenotaph, which is the national memorial to those who died in the First World War.

'An act of remembrance is an act of honour,'
said the Queen, 'to those who sacrificed all, who bore the
sufferings of war, who had the wisdom to build the peace.'

The Queen
introduced the
Elizabeth Cross, a medal
awarded to the families of
those who died on military
trips, giving special
recognition to their
deep loss.

The Royal Yacht Britannia

Sleek and elegant, the Royal Yacht Britannia swept smoothly and swiftly across the ocean.

For 44 years, Britannia was the royal palace at sea. First setting sail in 1953, it travelled more than one million nautical miles – once around the world for every year of the Queen's life. She described it as the one place in the world where she could truly relax.

The ship carried the Queen on overseas visits, and was an important symbol of the Commonwealth. She hosted official meetings and glittering state dinners from the ship. Although it was luxurious and relaxing, the Queen spent much of her time aboard hard at work, dealing with official matters and keeping up with her busy schedule.

Today the yacht is a tourist attraction in Edinburgh. All the clocks on board tell the same time – 3.01 p.m. – the moment the Queen stepped off for the last time, in December 1997.

43

Winston Churchill

Anthony Eden

Harold Macmillan

Alec Douglas-Home

Prime Ministers

Every Wednesday, the Queen would hold a weekly meeting with her current prime minister. Seated comfortably in armchairs, they could discuss anything. The details of the meeting were completely secret and no one else attended . . . except occasionally one of the corgis.

In Britain, as head of state, the Queen remained politically neutral. Although she didn't pass laws, she held a close and important relationship with government and with her prime ministers. Every time a new prime minister was elected, it was the Queen who officially invited them to form a government. She also delivered the Queen's Speech at every State Opening of parliament, outlining what the government would do.

During her reign, the Queen was served by fifteen different prime ministers and saw seventy years of changing political history.

What a wealth of perspective, experience and wisdom she was able to share.

John Major

Theresa May

Harold Wilson

Edward Heath

James Callaghan

Margaret Thatcher

Tony Blair

Gordon Brown

David Cameron

Boris Johnson

Liz Truss

The 2010s

A helicopter whirred as the iconic James Bond theme tune swirled around the Olympic stadium. The crowds gazed up in astonishment to see Her Majesty the Queen, accompanied by Secret Agent 007, dive out . . . and parachute gracefully to the ground. Moments later, as the Queen took her seat at the opening ceremony of the London 2012 Olympics, her face was enveloped in a wide smile.

The Olympic and Paralympic Games were a huge success for Britain. The country was swept up in feel-good energy and a sense of camaraderie that was infectious. As the Olympic torch was carried to all corners of the four nations, crowds turned out in great numbers to show support. Team GB went on to finish third in the medal table, winning more gold medals than Britain had collected for over one hundred years and creating a deep sense of excitement and national pride.

While the second half of the decade saw a country much divided over politics, the 2012 Olympics were an inspiring celebration of modern Britain, showcasing to the world a dynamic, innovative and inclusive nation with a strong spirit of togetherness.

And it all appeared to be kicked off by a daredevil stunt by the 86-year-old Queen. With a twinkle in her eye, she enjoyed showing the world her sense of fun.

On one memorable day of the Olympics, later called Super Saturday, Britain's athletes Mo Farah, Jessica Ennis and Greg Rutherford won three gold medals – a stunning celebration of the diversity and brilliance of British talent.

The Queen's Fashion

Amidst the crowds, there was a sudden flash of lemon yellow or fuchsia pink or emerald green . . . the Queen was on a walkabout and though small in size, she always stood out.

The Queen was very famous for her smart signature style. Bright and bold, her single-colour outfits celebrated all the colours of the rainbow and were matched with eye-catching brooches, a string of pearls and fabulous hats – frilled, flowered and feathered.

Her wedding gown was made from fabric bought using ration vouchers, just like the other dresses of the post-war era.

Although she was sometimes dressed in crowns and jewels, she was just as distinctive in her stylish everyday outfits.

Always impeccably turned out, the Queen's style was classic, timeless and utterly elegant.

The 2020s

Only one story dominated the start of the 2020s. A story that no one could have predicted or prepared for. Children's hand-drawn rainbows shone bravely from windows everywhere, as the shadow of the Covid-19 pandemic spread from country to country, causing disruption, hurt and heartbreak to thousands of people.

Friends and family were restricted from meeting and schools, offices, restaurants and shops shut their doors. The world went into lockdown to help protect lives.

During the pandemic, the Queen lost her beloved husband, Prince Philip, the Duke of Edinburgh. At his funeral she was required to sit alone as the world watched her mourn. It was an image of great sadness, but also of grace and quiet dignity.

In April 2020, in only her fifth televised speech aside from the annual Christmas broadcasts, the Queen addressed the nation from Windsor Castle. Into the distress and disorientation, she spoke words of comfort and courage.

DIEU ET MON DROIT

The Queen praised the valiant work of NHS frontline workers, care workers and emergency staff. She encouraged everyone to take pride in the small part they were playing for the greater good. She reminded everyone that they were united with nations across the whole world in a common goal.

Her Majesty's message was viewed live by 24 million people. It was a time of crisis in the life of the nation. But, just like the very first broadcast she had given with her sister when she was just fifteen, her speech touched the hearts of young and old. Her words rang out bright, determined and full of hope . . .

'Better days will return,' she promised. 'We will be with our friends again. We will be with our families again. We will meet again.'

The Queen and Prince Philip loved each other dearly. They were married for 73 years and the Queen referred to her husband as 'my strength and stay'.

Longest-Reigning Monarch

Regal and stately, a line of the longest-reigning monarchs winds through almost one thousand years of British history. Queen Elizabeth II holds the title of longest-serving sovereign and the first British monarch to celebrate a Platinum Jubilee.

These rulers span centuries of change and progress. Of war and peace. Of national joy . . . and sadness. Their reigns have seen invention and innovation, the development of science and medicine, the flourishing of art, music and literature.

Life was not always easy for those of their subjects who did not possess wealth, freedom or privilege. Yet the stories of these queens and kings are the stuff of history and of legend – to be heard for generations to come.

George III of
Great Britain

Victoria of
Great Britain

AJESTY THE QUEEN

James VI of Scotland /
James I of England

Henry III
of England

Edward III
of England

William I
of Scotland

Llywelyn of
Gwynedd

Elizabeth I
of England

David II
of Scotland

The Royal Jubilees

Flags fluttered and colourful bunting danced brightly
in the breeze on the Queen's Jubilee.

Royal jubilees celebrate the life and reign of a king or queen and the Queen's jubilees were marked with special services and celebrations throughout Britain. Tables were piled high with sandwiches, cakes and cups of tea as neighbours came together for festive street parties and special events.

For her Silver Jubilee (1977), marking 25 years on the throne, the Queen's royal carriage rolled smartly through many towns and cities across the United Kingdom. Crowds jostled gaily to catch a glimpse of the royal passenger and the Queen went on walkabouts, receiving posies of flowers and small gifts from children. She wanted to show how united the nation was and tried to see as many of her people as she could. She continued her tour across the Commonwealth, including visits to Australia, Tonga, Fiji and the Caribbean, travelling over 90,000 kilometres altogether.

·1977·

2002

During the Golden Jubilee (2002), celebrating fifty years, the Queen invited 500 members of the public, active in the community and from many different faiths, to a Jubilee Celebration. She used the words 'gratitude, respect and pride' to sum up how she felt about her people and the jubilee.

At the Diamond Jubilee (2012), celebrating sixty years, an array of brilliant boats bobbed merrily on the River Thames. The Queen joined a floating pageant of one thousand boats from the UK, Commonwealth and around the world. The celebrations also included a service at St Paul's Cathedral and the lighting of a chain of 4,200 bright beacons in countries all over the world.

Queen Elizabeth reigned for longer than any other British monarch and 2022 saw the nation commemorate her Platinum Jubilee – the first ever for a British king or queen. It marked seventy years on the throne.

The Queen celebrated by sharing a pot of tea with Paddington Bear.
A very royal tea party.

The Golden, Diamond and Platinum Jubilee celebrations included spectacular classical and pop concerts, featuring well-known musicians and singers.

The Green Queen

Oak and ash, copper beech and sweet chestnut, willow, cedar and birch.
With arms gently outstretched, a forest of green murmured and swayed,
reaching for the light. An abundance of beauty and breath.

Conservation and protection of the environment was always a concern
close to the heart of the Queen and her late husband Prince Philip.
Addressing the 26th UN Climate Change Conference in Glasgow
(COP26), Her Majesty urged the gathered leaders to 'create a safer,
stabler future for our people and the planet on which we depend.'
The Queen reminded them that:

'History has shown when nations come together in common cause
there is always room for hope . . . We are doing this not for ourselves
but for our children and our children's children and those
who will follow in their footsteps.'

Trees keep the climate and planet in balance and, to mark her Platinum Jubilee, Her Majesty launched the Queen's Green Canopy initiative. People planted trees across the UK and throughout the Commonwealth, with the Queen placing the very first in the grounds of Windsor Castle – just one of 1,500 trees she personally planted during her reign.

Woodland, avenues of trees and even single trees in people's back gardens were planted all over the UK, rejuvenating local ecosystems, boosting biodiversity, capturing carbon and creating new habitats for woodland creatures.

A living, breathing gift for future generations.

In 2018,
Sir David Attenborough
visited the Queen in
Buckingham Palace's gardens
to discuss conservation. Both
were 91 years old at the
time, and they chatted
and laughed like
old friends.

The Queen's Charities

Seated at row upon row of tables that stretched from Buckingham Palace to Trafalgar Square, 10,000 dripping-wet guests in white ponchos filled The Mall with laughter and merriment.

They went to have lunch with the Queen in honour of her ninetieth birthday and whilst the rain may have turned their sandwiches soggy, the very British weather did not dampen their spirits.

But the guests at this special lunch had more than matching rainwear and fine humour in common: they were each connected to one of 600 charities and organisations for which the Queen was patron.

Her Majesty supported the work of a wide range of organisations from across the UK and the Commonwealth. As their patron, the Queen made official visits to see their work, meeting staff, volunteers and the people they helped. She also hosted events for her charities at the royal palaces to celebrate their successes and reward their achievements.

Her Majesty's charities worked on many good causes close to the Queen's heart, including education, animals and wildlife conservation, faith, heritage, children's welfare, the environment, healthcare, science and technology, sport, the armed forces and the arts.

Supporting charities was a key part of the Queen's work and throughout her life she encouraged everyone to find ways to help make a difference for the greater good.

She leaves a remarkable legacy of kindness, care and compassion.

A visit from the Queen always created much buzz and excitement, and gave each organisation valuable publicity and recognition needed to carry on its work.

Remembering Our Queen

On her twenty-first birthday, with the world listening,
Princess Elizabeth made a solemn promise:

*'I declare before you all that my whole life, whether it be
long or short, shall be devoted to your service . . .'*

It was a promise she kept steadfastly throughout her
seventy-year reign as queen.

During that time, she inspired communities and countries to work together,
planted seeds of hope for future generations and encouraged
everyone to play their part in building a better world.

To the British people, she provided continuity, strength and stability in a rapidly
changing world. She shared in the nation's joys but also in its sorrows, always seeking
to rise above discord and difference. Always seeking to unite. In times of trouble,
it was often *her* words that shone out as a source of comfort and reassurance.

She did all this with quiet dignity, gentle humour and with a deep commitment
to family, country and God. Her life was an extraordinary example of service
to others and to public duty. Although frail, she performed official
tasks right until the last days of her life.

When Elizabeth II died, flags across the world flew at half-mast and a period of ten days mourning was observed. Tributes poured in from every corner of the globe for this revered head of state, shrewd diplomat, skilful ambassador and treasured monarch.

What a mark she leaves on history . . . Elizabeth, the girl who was never born to be queen – and yet became the greatest queen of all.

Elizabeth II
21 April 1926 – 8 September 2022

Glossary

Abdicate
To formally give up a position of authority or power. When a king or queen no longer wants to rule, they 'abdicate the throne'.

Abolish
To get rid of or put an end to something. This could be a law, a rule or a particular practice, such as apartheid.

Apartheid
A system of laws that forced black and white South Africans to live separately and took away the political rights of the majority black people. The word apartheid means 'apartness'.

Auxiliary Territorial Service (ATS)
The women's branch of the British Army during the Second World War. Although they were tasked with lots of vital roles during the war, women were not allowed to fight.

CBE
An award given by a reigning monarch for service to the community or a notable achievement. CBE stands for Commander of the British Empire.

Constitutional Monarchy
A type of government that has a king or queen at its head. The elected government rules the country but shares power with the monarch.

Commonwealth
An organisation of individual countries that are connected by choice and friendship for common good. Also called 'Commonwealth of Nations'.

Coronation
The grand, formal ceremony at which a person is crowned king or queen. During the ceremony the crown is placed on the new monarch's head and an oath is sworn.

Decimalisation
The term used for the process of moving to a new system of currency based on units of 10. UK currency went decimal on 15 February 1971.

Democracy
A type of government where the citizens can take an active part in making decisions on how a country is run. In a democracy, the people vote for who they want to lead their country.

Empire
A group of countries or territories invaded and ruled by another country. By 1922, the British Empire was the biggest in the world.

Gurkhas
Soldiers recruited from Nepal who serve in the British Army. They operate in many units, collectively known as The Brigade of Gurkhas.

Inherited

A title (such as queen) or goods received from a person who has died.

Immigration

The act of leaving your home country to start a new life in another country.

Jubilee

The celebration of a very special anniversary. Royal Jubilees celebrate the life and reign of a monarch, marking 25, 50, 60 and 70 years since they came to the throne.

KBE/DBE

Two honours given by a monarch, recognising inspirational contributions in any field of activity. KBE stands for Knighthood of the Order of the British Empire (for men) and DBE stands for Damehood of the Order of the British Empire (for women).

MBE

An award given by a reigning monarch to recognise outstanding achievement or service to the community. MBE stands for Member of the Order of the British Empire.

Monarchy

A form of government where one person, either a king or a queen, rules a nation. The United Kingdom is a constitutional monarchy, which means it has an elected government, but power is shared with the monarchy.

Oath

A formal promise to do a certain thing, usually spoken aloud and in front of other people.

OBE

An award given by a reigning monarch to recognise outstanding achievements in a person's area of work. OBE stands for Officer of the Order of the British Empire.

Pageant

A joyful and colourful parade or public performance, often celebrating a historical event.

Reconciliation

A process of restoring a good relationship between people or nations who have had differences, helping them to heal and understand each other.

Remembrance Sunday

Held on the second Sunday every November, a day for remembering those who lost their lives in world wars and other conflicts.

Sovereign

A leader who holds authority or absolute power, such as a king or a queen.

Subaltern

A junior officer in the British Army.

First published in Great Britain in 2022
by Wren & Rook

Text copyright © Smriti Prasadam-Halls, 2022
Illustration and design copyright
© Hodder and Stoughton Limited, 2022
All rights reserved.

The right of Smriti Prasadam-Halls, Kim Geyer and
Josie Shenoy to be identified as the author and illustrators
respectively of this Work has been asserted by them in
accordance with the Copyright, Designs & Patents Act 1988.

PB ISBN: 978 1 5263 6596 5
E-book ISBN: 978 1 5263 6600 9
10 9 8 7 6 5 4 3 2 1

Wren & Rook
An imprint of Hachette Children's Group
Part of Hodder & Stoughton
Carmelite House
50 Victoria Embankment
London EC4Y 0DZ

An Hachette UK Company
www.hachette.co.uk
www.hachettechildrens.co.uk

Printed in the United Kingdom

MIX
Paper from
responsible sources
FSC® C104740